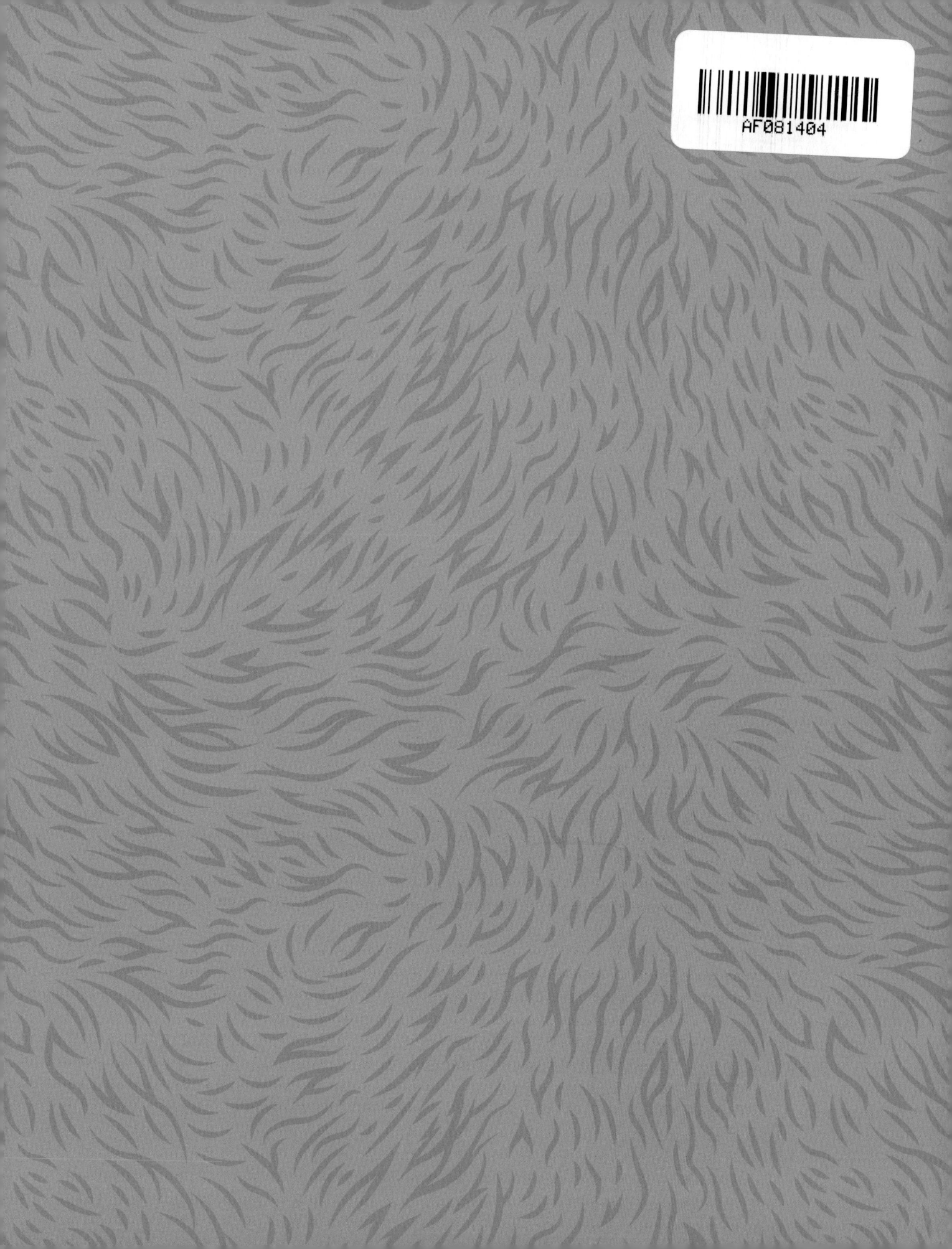

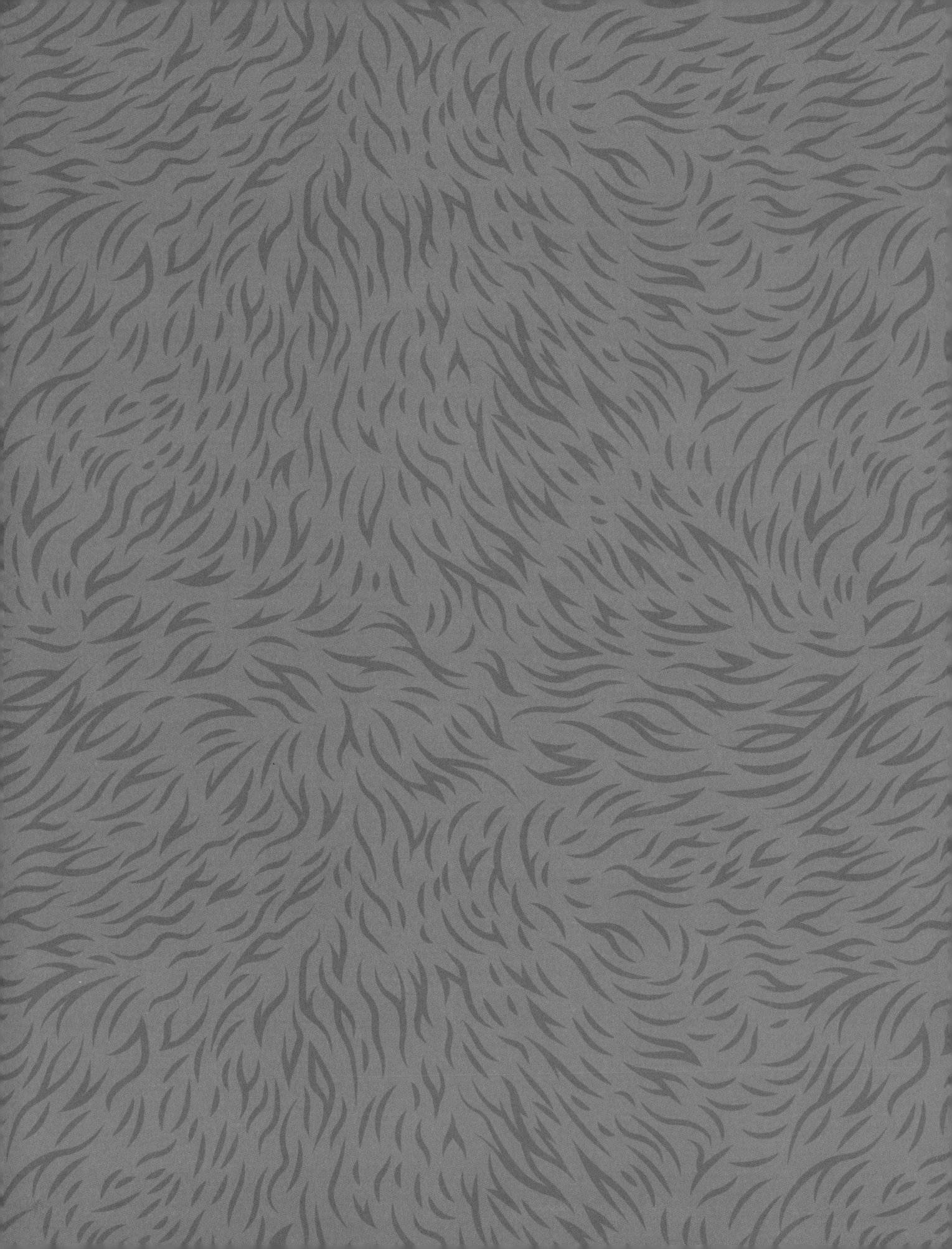

RECORD-BREAKING ANIMAL FACTS

And the SCIENCE behind them!

Izzi Howell

WAYLAND

First published in Great Britain in 2026 by Wayland
Copyright © Hodder & Stoughton Limited, 2026
Produced for Wayland by

All rights reserved.

Editor: Izzi Howell
Designer: Clare Nicholas

HB ISBN: 978 1 5263 2943 1
PB ISBN: 978 1 5263 2944 8

Wayland
An imprint of
Hachette Children's Group
Part of Hodder & Stoughton Limited
Carmelite House
50 Victoria Embankment
London EC4Y 0DZ

An Hachette UK Company
www.hachette.co.uk
www.hachettechildrens.co.uk

The authorised representative in the EEA is Hachette Ireland, 8 Castlecourt Centre, Dublin 15, D15 XTP3, Ireland (email: info@hbgi.ie)

FSC® MIX Paper | Supporting responsible forestry FSC® C104740 www.fsc.org

Printed in Dubai

Picture acknowledgements:
NASA: NASA/JPL-Caltech 17t; NOAA: NOAA Fisheries 19b; Shutterstock: Black Dingo, IdeaGeneration, Svetlana Foote, Yellow Cat, schankz, Harry Collins Photography, Eric Isselee, Coral Brunner, ANDRES MENA PHOTOS, Ajit S N and Hintau Aliaksei cover, Eric Isselee 3t and 16-17, Vaclav Volrab 3b and 26-27, slowmotiongli 4-5t and 31, D-sign Studio 10 4b, Elana Erasmus 5b, Friendly Studios 6l, myphotobank.com.au 6-7, Totostarkk9456 7r, Coral Brunner 8, MAHATHIR MOHD YASIN 9t, ianlusung 9b, Nikola Bilic 10l, alslutsky 10r, I Wayan Sumatika 11t, filkusto 11b, Henner Damke 12, Alexander_P 13t, Divelvanov 13b, Thorsten Spoerlein 14l and 30b, Rosa Jay 14-15, Refluo 15, Chantelle Bosch 16l, Monkey_Zen Studio and Fathur Kiwon 17b, Ajit S N 18-19, ghrzuzudu 19t, Jonathan Schaab 20, scott mirror 21t, Jrs Jahangeer and JUNIOR 319 21b, nvphoto 22, Manuel Balesteri 23t, burbura 23b, David Havel 24-25t and 30t, Philip Pilosian 24b, radoma 25b, Yulia Lakeienko 27t, White Space Illustrations 27b, Lauren Suryanata 28t, frank60 28c, Nicram Sabod 28b, ANDRES MENA PHOTOS 29t, Danny Ye 29c; Wikimedia: URSchmidt 29b.

All design elements from Shutterstock.

The website addresses (URLs) included in this book were valid at the time of going to press. However, it is possible that contents or addresses may have changed since the publication of this
book. No responsibility for any such changes can be accepted by either the author or the publisher.

All facts and statistics were correct at the time of press.

MEASUREMENTS

Keep track of all the measurements in the book with this handy guide!

cm = centimetre
m = metre
km = kilometre
g = gram
kg = kilogram

CONTENTS

Sprint at speed	4
Champion snoozer	6
Mighty muncher	8
Harmful hunter	10
Top twister	12
Powerful poison	14
Cool climber	16
Underwater roar	18
Need for speed	20
Super furry animal	22
Marathon migrator	24
Skilled sniffer	26
More incredible animal records	28
Glossary	30
Further information	31
Index	32

Guess what I'm good at!

SPRINT AT SPEED

FASTEST RUNNER

With a top speed of 114 km per hour, the **CHEETAH** is the clear-cut sprinting champion of the savannah ... and the fastest land animal anywhere on Earth! Almost every part of the cheetah's body is adapted for super speed.

The cheetah has long claws that dig into the ground as it runs, giving it grip and preventing it from slipping.

Its massive stride length of over 6 m is thanks to its long legs and flexible spine. At top speed, a cheetah can take 3 1/2 strides per second.

DID YOU KNOW?

To reach their top speed *at* top speed, cheetahs need to accelerate quickly! Scientists have discovered that they can increase their speed by 10 km per hour in one single stride!

Stand back, I'm speeding up!

The cheetah's large heart and lungs help oxygen reach its muscles quickly for a boost of energy.

SWEATY SPRINTERS

However, cheetahs can only maintain their incredible speed for a maximum of 200–300 m. Their super sprints make them so hot that if they were to run for longer, they wouldn't be able to cool down through panting or sweating.

QUICK CHASE

Speed isn't a cheetah's only weapon. Its amazing agility and long tail for balance help it make twists and turns to follow its prey of quick-footed antelope.

Cheetahs usually hunt during the day to avoid competition with other big cats, such as lions and leopards, that hunt in the evening and at night.

CHAMPION SNOOZER

MOST TIME SPENT ASLEEP

Even the doziest person would find it hard to beat a **KOALA** in a sleep-off! These snoozy marsupials can sleep up to 18 to 22 hours a day. The reason for these mega naps is connected to what they eat.

🍴 DIFFICULT DIET

Koalas are famously picky eaters. Their meal of choice? Eucalyptus leaves ... and lots of them! The only problem for koalas is that their favorite food doesn't really contain any nutrients or give them any energy.

The koala can eat up to 1 kg of eucalyptus leaves in just one day!

Food stays in the koala's digestive system for a long time, which helps them to extract every last drop of energy and nutrients from it.

Koalas often sit in the fork of a tree to keep safe while napping. They usually eat and sleep in the same tree to be extra efficient!

🌿 Extracting Energy

The koala's digestive system has to work really hard to break down eucalyptus leaves and extract the few nutrients they contain, which is tiring to begin with. The tiny amount of energy they do get from the leaves needs to be saved for important activities, like gathering more eucalyptus! So they save energy the rest of the time by taking a nice, long nap.

To make matters even trickier for koalas, eucalyptus leaves are actually poisonous. The koala's liver and special bacteria in their intestines work together to break down toxins from the leaves.

I don't need this, I just like the taste!

🏆 Did You Know?

Although eucalyptus doesn't give koalas much energy, it does provide them with plenty of liquid! This means they rarely need to drink any water.

Mighty MUNCHER

MOST POWERFUL BITE

Stay clear of the crushing jaws of the **SALTWATER CROCODILE**! Its jaws are almost four times stronger than those of other fearsome predators, such as lions or tigers. How do these scary snappers achieve such super strength?

- The short answer is ... muscle! Saltwater crocodiles have extra space in their skulls which is filled with powerful jaw muscles.

- The jaw muscles of the saltwater crocodile are very stiff and strong – almost as hard as bone.

- A second joint in their jaw helps distribute the force of the bite across the mouth, giving them mega-strength no matter where they grab their prey.

AMBUSH ATTACK

Saltwater crocodiles will eat almost anything that comes their way ... deer, wild boar, water buffalo or even humans! They ambush their prey and grip it hard to stop it from escaping.

Saltwater crocodiles swallow small prey whole ... gulp!

SPIN TO KILL

Funnily enough, saltwater crocodiles don't actually use their teeth to cut through large pieces of meat! Instead, they tear their prey into pieces using a gruesome 'death roll'. During a death roll, the crocodile clamps onto its prey with its jaws and teeth, and then spins around to rip it apart.

DID YOU KNOW?

The muscles that a crocodile uses to open its mouth are much weaker than those used to close its jaw. In theory, you could hold a crocodile's mouth shut with your hand, but **don't** try this at home!

I wouldn't risk it!

Harmful HUNTER

MOST SUCCESSFUL PREDATOR

What's the world's scariest predator ... maybe a great white shark? These toothy tyrants actually only manage to catch 50 per cent of the animals they chase. In contrast, the **DRAGONFLY** successfully hunts and kills a whopping 95 per cent of the prey it goes for! Who's scarier now?!

Dragonflies have some of the largest eyes of any insect. Their eyes take up almost their whole head, which gives them a full field of vision. All the better to spot their next victim!

Once a dragonfly has spotted its prey, it calculates the best flight path to ambush it in mid-air. It then races towards it at speeds of up to 48 km per hour (faster than the fastest humans can run!)

A DRAGONFLY'S DINNER

Dragonflies eat a wide variety of other insects, including flies, bees, butterflies and even smaller dragonflies. After they catch their prey, they carry it to a perch where they munch it down. Bon appetit!

Dragonflies usually catch small, flying prey.

Dragonflies use their incredible flying skills to chase their prey through the air. They can quicky change direction and even fly upside down and backwards, so there's no chance of escape!

SNEAKY SLOW MOTION

If we could see like a dragonfly, everything would look as if it were in slow motion! This is because dragonflies are able to see much faster than humans - around 200 images per second, compared to 60 for humans. This helps them react super quickly to their prey's movement.

DID YOU KNOW?

Each dragonfly eye is made up of around 28,000 tiny 'eyes' that contain light-sensitive cells.

All the better to see you with!

TOP TWISTER

MOST FLEXIBLE LIMBS

Each of the **OCTOPUS'** eight arms can move in many different ways and directions! Octopuses can bend, twist, shorten and lengthen their arms, moving them up, down, left and right, to name just a few examples. In one study, scientists counted over 16,500 different types of movement!

AMAZING ARMS

With the freedom to move their arms in so many different ways, it's unsurprising that octopuses use their limbs for a huge range of purposes, including swimming, catching prey, fighting other octopuses, walking along the sea bed and moving objects around!

Octopuses have soft bodies with no bones, so they aren't limited by the movement of their skeleton or joints.

Their arms are 'muscular hydrostats' – a fancy term for muscles with no bones inside (like our tongues). The muscles in each arm provide support for each other.

DID YOU KNOW?

Octopuses can taste their prey by touching it with their tentacles! Their suckers contain taste receptors, just like the ones on our tongues!

Mmmm delicious!

ESCAPE ARTISTS

Octopuses are very clever animals. Some that live in captivity often escape from their tanks by carrying out complex escape plans that make full use of their incredible flexibility. Some octopuses have even been known to break into other tanks to snack on the animals inside!

The underside of each arm is covered in suckers that use suction to attach to different surfaces or pick up objects. Octopuses contract and relax muscles in the suckers to attach and then let go.

Because of their soft bodies, octopuses can squeeze into very small spaces to take shelter or hide from predators.

POWERFUL POISON

MOST POISONOUS

Despite its small size of just 6 cm in length, this colourful rainforest dweller is considered to be the most poisonous animal on Earth. Just one tiny **GOLDEN POISON FROG** contains enough poison to kill ten adult men!

POISON VS VENOM

The golden poison frog is poisonous, which means that if you ate it, you'd be in big trouble. However, unlike venomous animals, it can't hurt you by biting you or stinging you.

The skin glands of the golden poison frog produce an incredibly powerful poison. It's so strong that even touching the frog can harm you.

Stand back!

The frog's bright colour warns predators of its terrible poison. Despite their name, golden poison frogs can actually be yellow, mint green or orange.

YOU ARE WHAT YOU EAT

The golden poison frog gets its poison from the insects it eats, which in turn, get them from the plants they eat. For this reason, golden poison frogs raised in captivity and fed different prey aren't poisonous at all.

DID YOU KNOW?

The poison from one golden poison frog could kill 20,000 mice!

Squ-eek!

The golden poison frog's deadly poison and cautionary colouring are so effective that barely any animals dare to eat it. However, a few species of snake have developed a resistance to its poison.

Cool CLIMBER

Slippery, polished glass? Vertical walls? Ceilings? You name it, the **GECKO** can climb across it! The secret to the gecko's climbing success lies in sticky pads found on its toes.

If you looked at a gecko's toe pad through a microscope, you'd see that it was covered in many hairlike strands with forked ends.

These strands fan out and cling to tiny irregularities found on a surface, creating a force that helps the gecko cling on.

The attraction force created between the gecko's toe pads and the surface it's on is so strong that a gecko can hang from just one toe without falling!

🧪 INSPIRING SCIENCE

Scientists and engineers have created new products inspired by gecko feet, including adhesive tape and a robot that can climb walls. Like gecko feet, these products also use tiny forked strands to cling to surfaces.

🫧 QUICK CLEAN

If a gecko gets dirt or sand in between its toe pads, it is much harder for it to climb, as the strands aren't able to cling on properly. Luckily, the gecko's toe pads are self-cleaning. All it takes is a few steps and the dirt and sand fall away!

NASA are developing robots with gripping technology inspired by gecko feet that can be used on the outside of space stations or even to explore planets.

🏆 DID YOU KNOW?

One of the only surfaces that geckos can't cling to is Teflon, a coating used on non-stick pans!

What's happening?!

UNDERWATER ROAR

LOUDEST ANIMAL

The **BLUE WHALE** is famous for being the largest animal of all time. However, it also holds another less well-known title - the loudest animal on Earth. Blue whales make sounds to communicate with each other across the oceans. The sounds they make are so loud, they can be heard up to 1,600 km away!

The sounds made by blue whales are so low that humans can't hear them. However, it's no problem for specially adapted blue whale ears.

Unlike humans, blue whales don't have vocal cords (flaps of tissue in the throat used to produce sound). Instead, they make sounds with their larynx (an organ at the top of their throat).

Blue whales make sounds to tell each other where food is located, if they are looking for a mate or to warn each other of danger. Watch out over there!

SEA SENSES

Hearing is a very important sense for many sea animals. Light and smells don't move well through the water, so animals can't always depend on seeing or smelling their surroundings. However, sound waves actually travel faster and further through water than through the air, making it the perfect way to communicate under the waves!

DID YOU KNOW?

The call of a blue whale can be as loud as a jet plane!

🔊 QUIETEN DOWN!

Scientists worry that noise pollution from ships is making it harder for blue whales to communicate with each other. The noise is also stressful for many animals and can affect their behaviour.

At nearly 30 m long, the blue whale is the loudest *and* the longest animal! What a champion!

NEED FOR SPEED

FASTEST ANIMAL

Although the cheetah is known for its incredible sprints on land, it isn't actually the overall speed champion. That title goes to a lesser-known candidate - the **PEREGRINE FALCON**. This bird of prey can dive at a maximum speed of 323 km per hour, making it the fastest animal on Earth!

The peregrine falcon hunts by flying high and then diving down to catch its prey. It's during these dives, which are known as stoops, that it reaches its top speed. Gravity from the dive helps to boosts its speed.

Like the cheetah, the peregrine falcon has big lungs and a large heart that help to pump lots of oxygen to its muscles so that it can fly even faster.

🪶 SMOOTH SAILING 🪶

Objects moving through the air are slowed down by air resistance (friction between the air and the object). To optimise its speed, the peregrine falcon has a streamlined silhouette and pointed wings, which help to reduce air resistance.

The peregrine falcon pulls in its wings during its dive to reduce air resistance further.

Strong flight muscles add huge amounts of power to the peregrine falcon's flight before it starts its dive. This helps it build up speed.

👁 EYES ON THE PRIZE

Semi-transparent extra 'eyelids' cover the peregrine falcon's eyes during its dive to protect them from wind and dust. This allows it to keep a good view of its prey as it speeds towards it!

 **DID YOU KNOW?**

At top speed, a peregrine falcon can easily move as fast as a Formula 1 racing car!

Can't keep up with me!

SUPER FURRY ANIMAL

THICKEST FUR

Unlike other marine creatures, **SEA OTTERS** don't have any blubber (fat) to keep them warm in the chilly northern waters of the Pacific Ocean. Instead, they rely on something much more snuggly - fur, and LOTS of it!

Sea otters actually have two layers of fur - a top layer of long, waterproof guard hairs and a bottom layer of thick fur for insulation.

'FUR' REAL?

The bottom layer of sea otter fur contains over 150,000 strands of hair per square cm. In comparison, your head only contains about 125 to 200 hairs per square cm.

Young sea otters have even thicker fur than adults. Their fur traps so much air that they can effortlessly float in the water while their mum dives to hunt for lunch.

The hairs in the sea otter's outer layer of fur are covered in tiny microscopic spikes. These help the hairs stick together so that no water can get past them.

GREAT GROOMERS 👍

Sea otters have to keep their outer layer of fur squeaky clean for it to remain waterproof. They groom themselves like cats, using their tongues and paws to wipe away any dirt. Their skin is very loose, so they can pull it around to help them reach tricky, hidden spots.

The bottom layer of fur is incredibly dense. It traps warm, dry air close to the skin to keep the sea otter nice and cosy!

DID YOU KNOW?

Sadly, sea otters' supersoft fur made them a popular target for hunters and they were nearly hunted to extinction. Luckily, thanks to hunting bans and conservation projects, their population is recovering.

Keep off my fuzzy fur!

MARATHON MIGRATOR

LONGEST MIGRATION

Plenty of animals migrate (travel to other areas, often with the seasons) but none of their journeys come close to the mega migrations of the **ARCTIC TERN**. These small but strong birds travel up to 70,000 km each year in their migrations back and forth between the Arctic and the Antarctic.

☀ SUMMER FOREVER?

The Arctic tern breeds in the Arctic during summer in the northern hemisphere. As summer ends, it heads down to the Antarctic to catch summer in the southern hemisphere, before heading back up to the Arctic again! In this way, it makes the most of each hemisphere's best weather and never has to suffer through an extreme polar winter with very little food to eat.

Arctic terns live and migrate in colonies. Just before they leave for migration, the entire colony falls silent so that all the birds can prepare to leave at the same time.

GONE WITH THE WIND

The Arctic tern's migration route doesn't take a straight route north or south. Instead, they fly in a curved path to take advantage of wind currents that will help carry them through the air.

The Arctic tern is very light, so it doesn't need to use up a lot of energy flapping hard to keep itself up in the air.

The Arctic tern's long, thin wings make it very aerodynamic. It easily glides on the wind, rather than having to push itself forwards by flapping.

Arctic terns can eat and even sleep while gliding through the air, so there's no need for them to stop for breaks.

DID YOU KNOW?

The distance travelled by an Arctic tern throughout its lifetime is about the same as three return trips to the Moon!

384,400 km

Skilled SNIFFER

BEST SENSE OF SMELL

Who's got the strongest sense of smell in the animal kingdom? Dogs? Rats? Think again! The unlikely champion is actually the **AFRICAN ELEPHANT!** The secret to their sniffing superpower doesn't just lie in the size of their nose, but also in tiny receptors found inside it.

The African elephant carries a record-breaking number of smell receptor genes. Smell receptors are the parts of the body responsible for picking up smells and sending information about them to the brain via the nervous system.

Scientists believe that the African elephant's sense of smell is twice as powerful as that of a dog and five times more powerful than that of a human.

As well as being able to identify tons of different smells, the African elephant can also remember certain smells for long periods of time, thanks to their incredible memory.

SNIFFING OUT SNACKS

African elephants use their superior sense of smell to find their favourite food of trees and shrubs, and watering holes where they can drink.

FINDING FRIENDS

They can also use smell to learn more about other elephants, including their age, health and gender. They can even sniff out which elephants are related to them and identify strange elephants that don't belong to their herd.

When elephants meet, they often flap their ears at each other. It is believed that this is a way of pushing their scent towards each other so they can learn more about who they have met.

DID YOU KNOW?

Scientists think that it might be possible to train elephants to sniff out certain diseases in people!

Smells like a cold to me!

MORE INCREDIBLE

LARGEST EARS BY SIZE

With a name like the **LONG-EARED JERBOA**, it's no surprise that this animal has some seriously big ears! Its ears are about two-thirds of the length of its body – just imagine what that would look like on a human! The large size of its ears helps to release heat from its body so that it can stay cool in its desert habitat.

DEADLIEST TO HUMANS

The tiny **MOSQUITO** may be small in size, but its bite is incredibly dangerous. When mosquitoes bite humans to drink their blood, they can pass on deadly diseases, such as malaria. These diseases kill between 725,000 to 1,000,000 people every year, making the mosquito the deadliest animal on Earth.

STRONGEST MATERIAL PRODUCED BY AN ANIMAL

Scientists have discovered that the **LIMPET**'s teeth are the strongest material produced by an animal, beating spider silk and many other human-made materials! The strength of their teeth comes from iron and tiny mineral fibres found inside them. So, what do limpets do with their superstrong teeth? Scrape algae off rocks to eat ... yum!

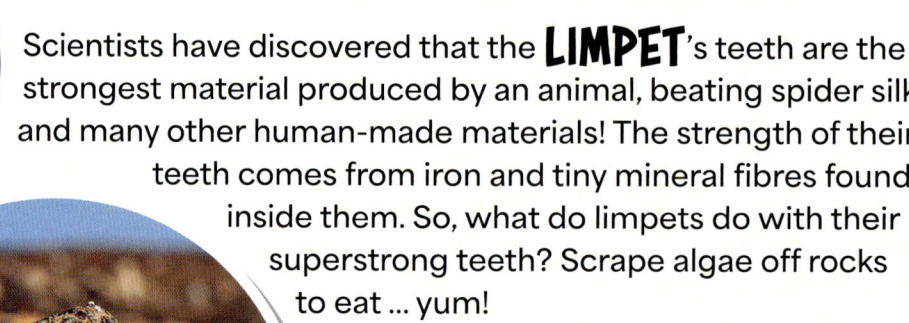

ANIMAL RECORDS

HIGHEST FLYING

This adventurous bird has been found flying at 11,300 m above sea level, which is as high as a commercial aeroplane! The **RÜPPELL'S VULTURE**'s blood is adapted to absorb more oxygen from the air, which means that it can survive in the low levels of oxygen at high altitudes.

MOST ELECTRIC

The **ELECTRIC EEL** can send out jolts to stun their prey that are more powerful than the electricity produced by any other animal. Their electricity is generated in a special organ that contains power-storing cells (a bit like batteries).

STRONGEST BY SIZE

One species of **DUNG BEETLE** can pull an incredible 1,141 times its own body weight. That's the equivalent of a human lifting six double decker buses! Its strength is very important, as males fight each other to decide who gets to mate. Only the strongest are successful!

Who fancies an arm wrestle?

GLOSSARY

aerodynamic something that is well suited to moving through the air

cell the smallest part of a living thing

conservation protecting animals, plants and the natural habitats where they live

genes units of genetic material (usually DNA) that contain instructions for how a living thing develops, grows and functions

glide to fly by floating instead of using power from wings or an engine

hemisphere one half of Earth – the Northern Hemisphere is located above the equator and the Southern Hemisphere is located below the equator

insulation a covering that stops heat from escaping or entering

marsupial a type of mammal that gives birth to its young before they are completely developed, such as a kangaroo

mate an animal with which another animal reproduces and has babies; to reproduce with another animal

migrate to travel to a new place, often when the season changes

oxygen a gas found in the air that cells need to produce energy

poisonous describes something that is dangerous if you eat it or if it gets into your body

predator an animal that hunts and kills other animals for food

prey an animal that is eaten by other animals

streamlined describes something with a smooth shape

venomous describes something that attacks by biting or stinging to inject a harmful or toxic substance

Further Information

Books

Curious Nature: Animals by Nancy Dickmann
(Franklin Watts, 2020)

You Choose: Animals by Izzi Howell
(Wayland, 2024)

Zany, Brainy Animals series by Ashley Ward and Andy Rowland
(Wayland, 2024)

Websites

Learn more about some of the fastest animals in the world
www.livescience.com/59822-fastest-animals.html

Find out more about cute and cuddly sea otters
kids.nationalgeographic.com/animals/mammals/facts/sea-otter

Get more information about amazing animal migrations
www.bbc.co.uk/bitesize/articles/zrt66g8#zpd88hv

Those websites look roar-some!

Index

air resistance 21
Arctic terns 24-25

bite 8, 28
blue whales 18-19
bones 8, 12

cheetahs 4-5, 20
claws 4
climbing 16, 17
colours 15

diving 20, 21, 23
dragonflies 10-11
dung beetles 29

ears 18, 27, 28
electric eels 29
elephants 26-27
eyes 10, 11, 21

flying 10, 11, 20, 21, 25, 29
food 6, 7, 9, 11, 13, 15, 18, 24, 25, 27, 28
fur 22, 23

geckos 16-17
golden poison frogs 14-15

hearing 18, 19
heart 5, 20

koalas 6-7

limpets 28
long-eared jerboas 28
lungs 5, 20

migration 24, 25
mosquitoes 28
muscles 5, 8, 9, 12, 13, 20, 21

octopuses 12-13
oxygen 5, 20, 29

peregrine falcons 20-21
poison 7, 14, 15
predators 8, 10, 13, 15
prey 5, 8, 9, 10, 11, 12, 15, 20, 21, 29

Rüppell's vultures 29

saltwater crocodiles 8-9
sea otters 22-23
skin 14, 23
sleeping 6, 7, 25
smell 19, 26, 27
sound 18, 19
speed 4, 5, 10, 20, 21
strength 8, 9, 28, 29

teeth 9, 28

TITLES IN THE SERIES

- Sprint at speed
- Champion snoozer
- Mighty muncher
- Harmful hunter
- Top twister
- Powerful poison
- Cool climber
- Underwater roar
- Need for speed
- Super furry animal
- Marathon migrator
- Skilled sniffer
- More incredible animal records

- Diverse dinos
- Bone-crushing bite
- Baby brain
- Claw-some lengths
- Small-o-saurus
- Too many teeth?
- Sturdy skulls
- Number one dino
- Tail titan
- Mum's the word
- Crest champion
- Bonkers big
- More incredible dinosaur records

- Explosive eruption
- Wave power
- Dusty and dry
- So many species
- Speedy breeze
- Mighty mountain
- Cool as ice
- Burn, baby, burn
- Champion coral
- Dark depths
- Waterfall wonder
- Plant power
- More incredible Earth records

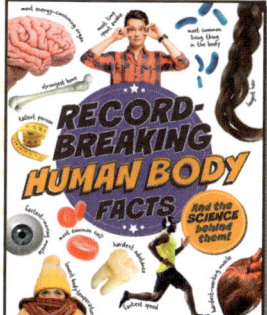

- Prize-winning pumping
- Feeling sleepy?
- Brain drain
- Almost freezing
- Mega-fast muscle
- So many cells
- Not so small
- Deep breath in ...
- Hard as a ... tooth?
- Rocket-powered run
- Baby bones
- Body invaders
- More incredible human body records

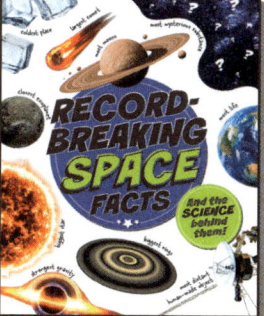

- A real superstar
- Short days
- Far, far away
- A powerful pull
- Roaming robots
- Mega rings
- Alive and kicking
- Space neighbour
- Strange substance
- Hot and cold
- So many moons
- Life lift-off
- More incredible space records

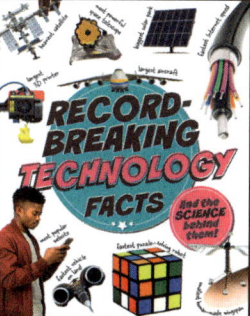

- Too big to fly?
- Champion clicks
- Deep, deep down
- Solid and sturdy
- Prize processors
- Let it shine
- (Nearly!) supersonic speed
- Seeing in space
- Fabulous fliers
- King of the printers
- Whizzy WiFi
- Super satellite
- More incredible technology records

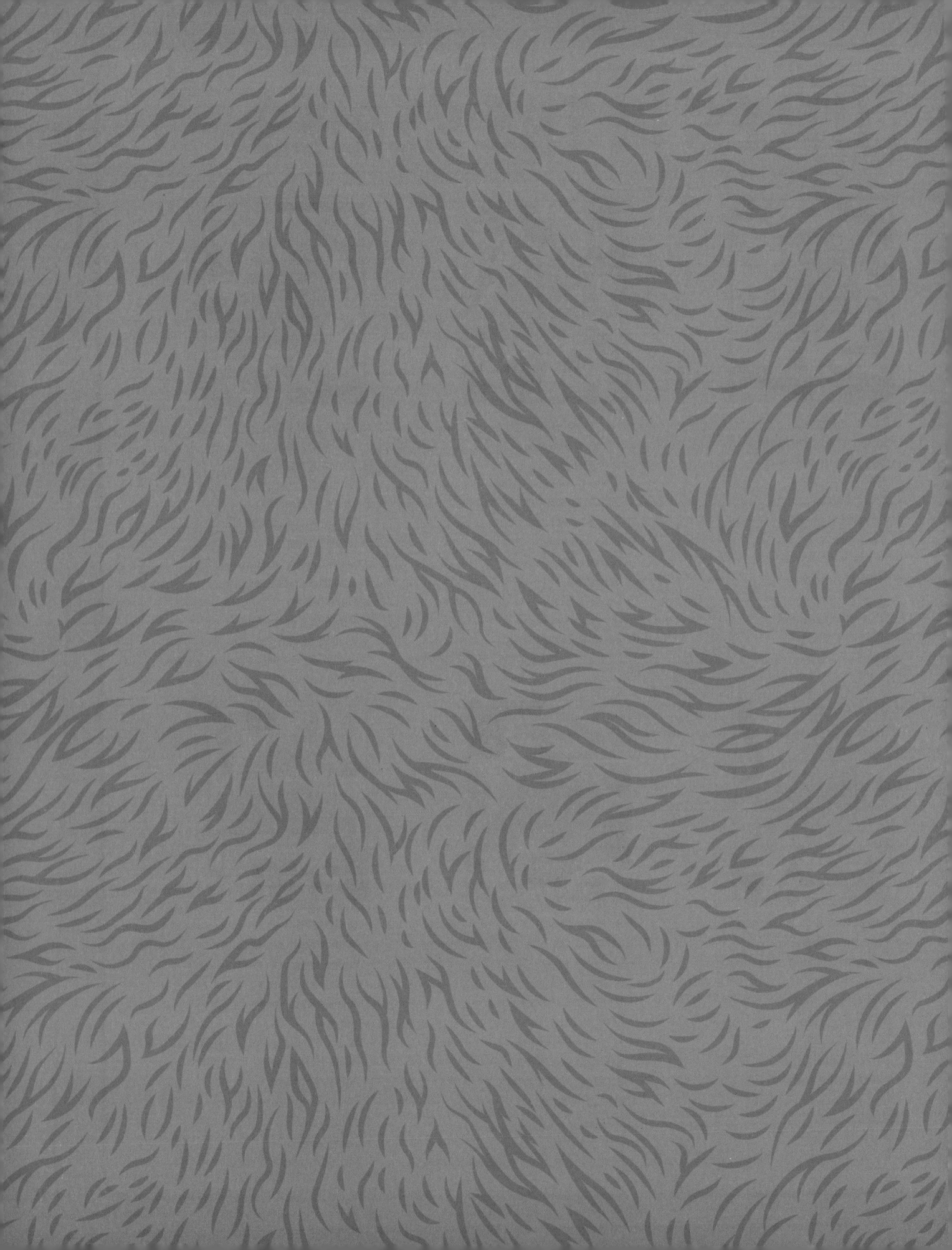